CONTENTS

ABOUT ME

WELCOME TO MY DIY HACK JOURNAL!

I'm Kirsty Griffiths, and I'm thrilled to embark on this creative journey with you. Over the past eight years, I've immersed myself in the world of DIY, transforming spaces and tackling projects that have brought both joy and challenges. This journal is a culmination of those experiences, filled with the insights, tips, and hacks that I've gathered along the way.

Whether you're a seasoned DIY enthusiast or just beginning your home improvement adventure, this journal is designed to inspire and guide you. From planning and designing to executing your dream projects, I'm here to share my passion and help you turn your visions into reality. Each page is crafted with care, offering practical advice, step-by-step instructions, and a sprinkle of creativity to spark your imagination.

A few years ago, I realised the importance of documenting everything I've learned over the past eight years of creating DIY hacks to help others. After completing our recent home extension, I saw it as my chance to take the lead. There are countless decisions and agreements to make during a home renovation. Whether you're just starting your renovation journey, the builders have left and you're ready to design your interior, or you're simply looking to upgrade areas in your home, I'm here to assist you.

Effective planning is essential in any DIY project, and I'll share my favourite hacks, insights on design, and planning tips to help you create your dream home.

While I may not be a guru, I hope to be your guide on your latest DIY project.

Join me as we explore the endless possibilities of DIY. Let's roll up our sleeves, grab our tools, and create something amazing together!

 www.kirstygriffiths.co.uk

www.instagram.com/griffiths_kirsty

www.youtube.com/@kirstygriffiths749

WHAT IS A DIY HACK?

WHAT IS A DIY HACK?

A DIY (Do-It-Yourself) hack is a creative and innovative way to modify, repurpose, or enhance an existing item or space. The term "hack" refers to a clever solution or ingenious method that simplifies a task or improves functionality. DIY hacks often involve using readily available materials and tools to achieve a unique and personalised result.

THE ESSENCE OF A DIY HACK

- **Creativity:** DIY hacks are all about thinking outside the box. They require a creative mindset to see the potential in everyday items and transform them into something extraordinary.
- **Resourcefulness:** These projects often involve repurposing materials or finding alternative uses for items you already have. This not only saves money but also promotes sustainability.
- **Customisation:** One of the main appeals of DIY hacks is the ability to tailor projects to your specific needs and preferences. Whether it's customising furniture to fit a particular space or adding personal touches to decor, DIY hacks allow for complete personalisation.
- **Problem-Solving:** Many DIY hacks stem from the need to solve a problem or improve functionality. For example, turning an old ladder into a stylish bookshelf or converting a dresser into a bathroom vanity.

CONCLUSION

A DIY hack is a creative and resourceful way to enhance or repurpose existing items, adding a personal touch and solving practical problems. Through my Instagram and YouTube channel, I share my passion for DIY, providing inspiration, detailed tutorials, and a platform for engaging with fellow enthusiasts. Whether you're a seasoned DIYer or just starting out, I invite you to join me on this exciting journey of creativity and innovation.

ABOUT THIS BOOK

Welcome to the world of creative transformations with IKEA hacks! I'm thrilled to share my journey with you through my new IKEA hacks book. Over the years, I've discovered the joy and satisfaction that comes from turning simple, everyday furniture into unique and stylish pieces that truly reflect our personalities and needs. This book is a culmination of countless projects, each one a testament to the endless possibilities that a bit of creativity and some basic tools can unlock.

My passion for DIY projects began with a desire to make our living space more functional and aesthetically pleasing without breaking the bank. IKEA's affordable and versatile furniture provided the perfect canvas for my experiments. After sharing my hacks on YouTube and Instagram, I received an overwhelming response from people eager to try these projects themselves. This book is a response to that enthusiasm—a guide to help you embark on your own DIY adventures.

In this book, I aim to show you that anyone can create beautiful, customized furniture with a bit of imagination and effort. You don't need to be a professional carpenter or designer. With step-by-step instructions, practical tips, and a touch of creativity, you can transform basic IKEA pieces into bespoke items that enhance your home's style and functionality. If I can do it anyone can!

Whether you're a seasoned DIY enthusiast or just starting out, this book is designed to inspire and guide you. Each project is broken down into manageable steps, complete with detailed instructions, photos, and tips to ensure your success. From planning and designing to executing and finishing, I'm here to share my knowledge and passion with you. My goal is to empower you to take on these projects with confidence and enjoy the process as much as the end result.

This book is your guide to simplicity and savings! Inside, you'll find my top 5 hacks laid out in detail, complete with precise measurements, my unique methods, and design insights. I've already navigated the trial and error—cutting wood to the wrong size, crafting pieces that didn't quite fit—so you don't have to. By sharing my mistakes, I aim to save you both time and money. Dive in and discover how to avoid the pitfalls and achieve success in your projects!

MY FAVORITE 5 HACKS

Let's dive into the details! I've stumbled through the mistakes, squandered some cash, and ultimately discovered the most efficient ways to hack these items right at home. In this section, I've meticulously recorded all my measurements and shared my exclusive designs just for you to explore and use.

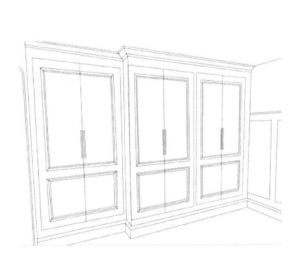

BILLY BOOKCASE HACK

MY FAVORITE IKEA HACK !

BILLY BOOKCASE

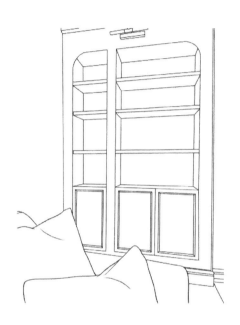

TRANSFORMING A BILLY BOOKCASE MY ULTIMATE IKEA DIY HACK:

If there's one thing I've learned from my years of DIY adventures, it's that even the most basic pieces of furniture can be transformed into something extraordinary with a little creativity and effort. One of my favorite projects has been hacking the iconic IKEA Billy Bookcase to create a custom piece that fits perfectly into my home's aesthetic.

Out of all the DIY projects I've undertaken, my IKEA Billy Bookcase hack stands out as my absolute favorite. This project not only transformed a simple piece of furniture into a stunning centerpiece but also allowed me to exercise creativity and craftsmanship in ways I hadn't before.

BEFORE I BUILT MY PAX:

When we were planning our big kitchen extension, I knew I wanted to build a fireplace with display cabinets on either side to create a focal point in what would be a very large room. I first picked up a second-hand fire surround on Facebook Marketplace for just £5. Once I had the fire surround, I could determine the size of the faux fireplace stack I needed to build. This may seem like an unconventional approach, but since we were working with an empty rectangular room, I could design the space around the fire surround.

We enjoyed one Christmas with our tree in the left-hand gap before I started building the built-in bookcase. I was eager to get the tree back in the loft and begin construction.

To get an idea of the costs involved, I contacted a few companies to inquire about having the bookcase built professionally. The lowest quote I received was £1500. While I knew that having it built by an expert would result in a stunning piece, it was simply out of my budget.

BILLY BOOKCASE

THE INSPIRATION

The adventure started when I came across some IKEA Billy bookcases on Facebook Marketplace. I saw potential in these second-hand units and decided to pair them with new Billy bookcases from IKEA to create a cohesive and expansive storage solution.

The first step was to prepare the bookcases for customisation. I didn't attach the back panel to each bookcase. To add a personal touch, I wallpapered the wall, giving the units a unique and stylish backdrop for my books and decor items.

I used this panelling wallpaper in my laundry room! It's fully paintable and super easy to put up.

THE INSPIRATION

The Billy Bookcase is a staple in many homes due to its affordability and versatility. However, I wanted to take it a step further and turn it into a piece that not only serves its functional purpose but also stands out as a unique design element in my living room. I envisioned a built-in look that would blend seamlessly with the rest of my decor while providing ample storage.

MATERIALS NEEDED

- Billy Bookcase (or multiple, depending on your space)
- MDF boards or trim
- Wood filler
- Sandpaper
- Primer and paint
- paint brushes
- Decorators Caulk
- Screws and brackets
- Tools: drill, saw, and a spirit level

BILLY
40x28x202 cm

ARTICLE NO: 502.638.38

PANELLING WALLPAPER
from Amazon

MDF DOORS
I made my own doors using
MDF & pine mouldings

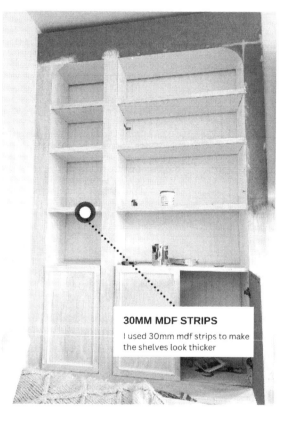

30MM MDF STRIPS
I used 30mm mdf strips to make
the shelves look thicker

BILLY BOOKCASE

STEP-BY-STEP PROCESS

I added 3cm thin MDF strips to make the shelves look thicker!

1. ASSEMBLY

First, I assembled the Billy Bookcase according to IKEA's instructions. This step is straightforward and sets the foundation for the hack.

3. PANELLING WALLPAPER

Paneling wallpaper is an excellent way to add some additional detail to the back of the Billy bookcase. It creates a textured, sophisticated look that enhances the overall design. Moreover, it's fully paintable, allowing you to customise the colour to perfectly match your decor.

4. CUSTOMISATION WITH TRIM

To achieve a built-in look, I added MDF boards and trim to the top, sides, and bottom of the bookcase. This created the illusion of a custom-built unit. The key here is to measure carefully and ensure all pieces fit snugly. I used no-more nails to attach.

5. FILLING AND SANDING

Next, I filled any gaps or screw holes with wood filler. Once dry, I sanded the entire surface to create a smooth finish. This step is crucial for achieving a professional look.

6. PRIMING AND PAINTING

I applied a coat of primer to help the paint adhere better. Once the primer dried, I painted the bookcase in a colour that matched the rest of my decor. I chose a classic white for a clean and timeless look, but you can opt for any colour that suits your style.

7. SECURING THE BOOKCASE

To ensure stability, I secured the bookcase to the wall using brackets. This is especially important if you have children or pets, as it prevents the unit from tipping over.

8. FINISHING TOUCHES

Finally, I caulked any remaining gaps between the bookcase and the wall to complete the built-in illusion. I also added decorative elements like crown moulding to enhance the overall appearance.

BILLY BOOKCASE

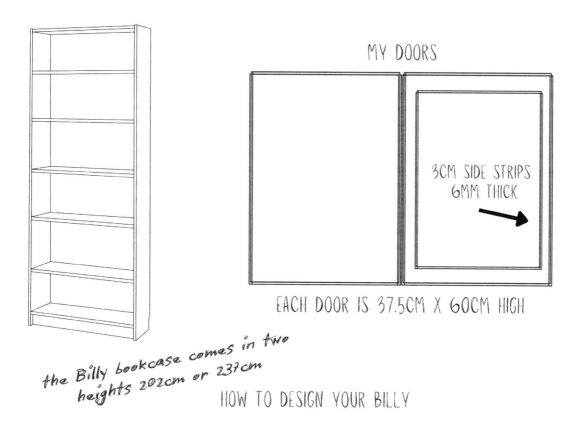

MY DOORS

3CM SIDE STRIPS
6MM THICK

EACH DOOR IS 37.5CM X 60CM HIGH

the Billy bookcase comes in two heights 202cm or 237cm

HOW TO DESIGN YOUR BILLY

- Measure the width, height, and depth of the space where you plan to place the bookcase.
- Note any architectural features such as windows, doors, or skirting boards that may affect the placement.
- Decide what you intend to store in the bookcase: books, decorative items, storage boxes, etc.
- Consider the weight and size of the items to ensure the shelves can accommodate them.
- IKEA offers Billy bookcases in various sizes and colors. Choose the base units that best fit your space and aesthetic.
- Consider if you need additional height extenders or corner units to maximize storage.
- Decide if you want to add doors to your bookcase for a cleaner look or to hide clutter.
- IKEA offers different door styles and finishes to match your preferences.
- Customize the number and placement of shelves according to your storage needs.
- Adjustable shelves offer flexibility for storing items of various heights.
- For additional storage options, consider adding drawers or cabinet inserts.
- These can be useful for storing smaller items or keeping certain belongings out of sight.
- Add LED lighting strips or spotlights to enhance visibility and highlight your displayed items.
- Consider IKEA's integrated lighting solutions.

BILLY BOOKCASE DOORS

IKEA offers a range of ready-to-fit doors that are both stylish and convenient.

If my ceilings had been taller and I had used the taller Billy units, I would have opted for the IKEA Billy doors.

- These doors are designed to perfectly complement the Billy system, providing a seamless and elegant finish.

Creating your own Billy bookcase doors can be a rewarding DIY project:
- Adds a personal touch to your furniture.

For my project, I used:
- 12mm MDF, cut to the perfect size to fit my bookcase.

To enhance the aesthetic appeal:
- Added a thin edge around the perimeter of each door.
- Included a thin strip for additional detail.

For functionality and style:
- Purchased soft close hinges from Amazon. Ensures the doors close smoothly and quietly.

Chose elegant gold handles, also from Amazon.
- Adds a touch of sophistication and complements the overall design beautifully.

This project not only improved the functionality of my bookcase but also gave it a unique, custom look that reflects my personal style (and loads of hidden storage)

For a more detailed explanation: Check out my YouTube video where I walk through the entire process step-by-step.

BILLY BOOKCASE

I MADE MY OWN DOORS

BILLY BOOKCASE

When planning the size of the MDF pieces to clad the unit I like to always make slightly smaller, its easier to fill a gap then try and trim yourself.

CEILING HEIGHT 235CM

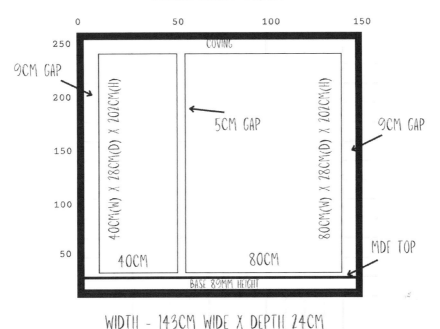

9CM GAP

5CM GAP

9CM GAP

40CM(W) X 28CM(D) X 202CM(H)

80CM(W) X 28CM(D) X 202CM(H)

COVING

MDF TOP

40CM

80CM

BASE 89MM HEIGHT

WIDTH - 143CM WIDE X DEPTH 24CM

BASE SIZE
C16 CLS TIMBER (L)2.4M (W)89MM (T)38MM

28CM X 143CM

BILLY BOOKCASE

STEP-BY-STEP INSTALLATION GUIDE

1. Fit Everything First: Ensure that all components are properly fitted and secured in their designated places.
2. Build the Wooden Frame: Once everything is in place, proceed to construct your wooden frame around the fitted components.
3. Measure for MDF Pieces: Only after the frame is built should you measure the exact dimensions needed for your MDF pieces. This ensures a precise fit and reduces the risk of measurement errors.

TIPS AND TRICKS

- Measure Twice, Cut Once: Precision is key when adding trim and MDF boards. Always double-check your measurements before cutting.
- Prep is Crucial: Don't skip the filling and sanding steps. They make a significant difference in the final finish.
- Choose Quality Paint: Investing in high-quality paint will ensure a smooth and durable finish.

THE RESULT

The transformation was remarkable. What started as a simple Billy Bookcase turned into a custom-built-in unit that added both functionality and style to my living room. The additional trim and paint elevated the piece, making it look far more expensive and bespoke than it actually was.

CONCLUSION

This Billy Bookcase DIY hack was not only fun to execute but also incredibly rewarding. It's amazing how a few modifications can transform a piece of basic furniture into something truly unique and tailored to your home. I hope this inspires you to take on your own DIY projects and see the potential in even the simplest pieces. Happy hacking!

Check out my youtube channel for my step-by-step guide

DESIGNING SHEET

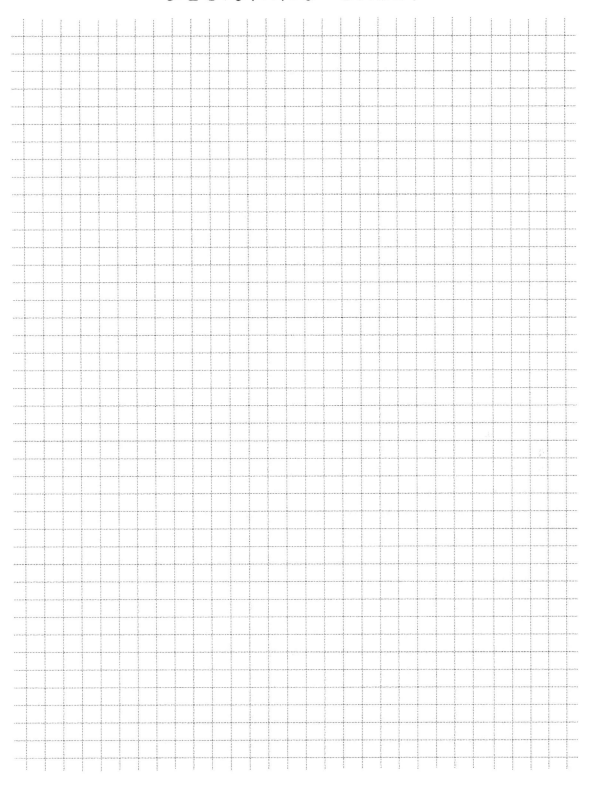

PROJECT PLANNER

Project Name

Start Date

End Date

Project Description

Must have features

Shopping list

Ideas & Notes

WARDROBE HACK

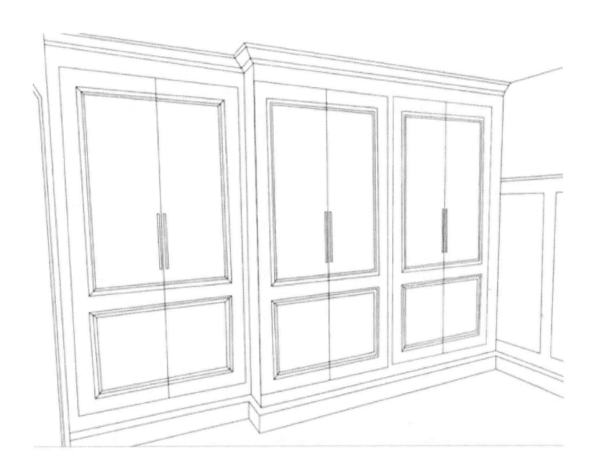

THESE WARDROBES TRANSFORMED OUR LIFE!

IKEA PAX WARDROBE

CREATING A BESPOKE WARDROBE FOR MY HUSBAND USING IKEA PAX UNITS

Every DIY project starts with an idea, a vision of what could be. For me, the journey of transforming standard IKEA Pax units into custom-built wardrobes began with a desire to create a functional yet stylish storage solution that would seamlessly blend into my home's decor.

It all started one afternoon as I stood in my bedroom, staring at the blank wall and the cluttered floor space. I knew I needed a change, something that would not only organise my husband's belongings but also add a touch of elegance to the room. That's when the idea struck me:

I could hack IKEA Pax units to create bespoke wardrobes tailored to my space as I'd done on the other side of my bedroom a year earlier. I talked it through with my husband as he'd always been hesitant to build a permanent structure along this wall, but with his clothes spilling out all over the floor he agreed I should build it. My husband tends to leave the DIY to me, but, I do always ask him what he thinks and he has given me some very good ideas. He trusts me.

Armed with a vision, I turned to my trusted resource for inspiration and guidance - INSTAGRAM.

Once I was inspired, I used the IKEA Pax Planner tool, which became my best friend, allowing me to experiment with different layouts and configurations until I found the perfect design. I had a door in the way! How would I make this all work? We then worked out that we could use the shallow depth pax, this would allow for the door to open and we still have some great storage!

With a clear plan in mind, I headed to IKEA and picked up the Pax wardrobe frames, doors, and a variety of internal fittings. The assembly of the units was straightforward, but the real magic began when I started customising them.

I meticulously measured the space, taking into account the non-standard ceiling heights and the existing skirting boards that I wanted to preserve. I cut MDF boards and trimmed them to size, label each piece to ensure everything fits perfectly.

IKEA PAX WARDROBE

The first step was building a base to raise up the pax wardrobes to allow me to run a skirting board across the front to really get a bespoke look as I'd done on my other wardrobes. I then started assembling the Pax units and securing them to the wall. Using screws, and my trusty drill, I ensured the frames were stable and level. This part of the project required patience and precision, but the effort was worth it. I then added the översidan lighting.

With the basic structure in place, it was time to add the finishing touches that would transform the wardrobes from standard to spectacular. I added a wooden frame and mdf strips cut to size around the edges of the units, creating a seamless built-in look. After filling in any gaps and screw holes with wood filler, I sanded the surfaces for a smooth finish. Then came the painting. I chose good old brilliant white dulux paint for wood to matched my bedroom decor, applying multiple coats of primer and paint to achieve a flawless look. I made sure I went through this in detail in my YouTube video. I then added pine moulding to the doors in a style i'd used before. If defiantly gave it a bespoke look.

The final steps involved installing the door handles , coving and attaching the skirting boards. These small details made a big difference, giving the wardrobes a polished and professional appearance. The handles were a real find on Amazon !

Standing back and looking at the finished product, I couldn't help but feel a sense of accomplishment. What started as a simple idea had turned into a beautiful, functional piece of furniture that added both style and organisation to my bedroom. The custom-built wardrobes not only provided ample storage but also enhanced the overall aesthetic of the room.

Throughout this journey, I faced challenges, like working with non-standard ceiling heights, wonky floors, and doing the one job I absolutely hate! adding coving to the top, i'm really not very good at doing it, it takes me ages, but I kept going and managed it. Installing coving can be quite the challenge! If you're looking for some extra support, I recommend checking out YouTube. You'll find fantastic guides and how-to videos on fitting coving from others who have mastered the craft!"

IKEA PAX WARDROBE

IF YOU'RE CONSIDERING A SIMILAR PROJECT, HERE ARE A FEW TIPS:

- Plan Thoroughly: Use tools like the IKEA Pax Planner.to visualise your design and ensure accuracy.
- Measure Carefully: Precision is key when customising and cutting materials.
- Invest in Quality: High-quality paint and materials make a significant difference in the final look.
- Take Your Time: Patience and attention to detail are crucial for a professional finish.

CONCLUSION

My IKEA Pax wardrobe hack was more than just a DIY project; it was a transformative journey that showcased the power of creativity and resourcefulness. By sharing my experience in this book, I hope to inspire others to take on their own DIY ventures and see the potential in everyday items. Remember, with a bit of imagination and effort, you can turn any space into something extraordinary.

IKEA PAX WARDROBE INFO

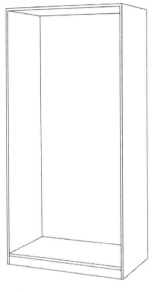

SHOPPING LIST

- 2 x IKEA Billy Bookcase 100x58x201 cm
- 1 x IKEA Billy Bookcase 100x35x201 cm
- 9 x KOMPLEMENT Soft closing hinge
- 6 x FORSAND Door, white stained oak effect, 50x195 cm
- MDF 18mm Boards (for custom trim and shelving)
- Wood Filler (to fill gaps and screw holes)
- Primer (for preparing surfaces before painting)
- Paint (Brilliant White Dulux paint for wood)
- Pine Moldings (for door and decorative accents)
- Coving (for the top edges)
- Skirting Boards (for the bottom edges)
- Screws
- 6 x Gold Door Handles (Amazon)

I've built the new 2.0 Pax unit in under 9 minutes

MOULDING & DOOR INFO

For my custom IKEA PAX project, I incorporated a few key elements to achieve a polished and professional look.
I purchased the pine moulding from B&Q. This type of moulding added a bespoke feel to the bookcase.

To attach the moulding, I used "No More Nails" adhesive. This product provided a strong and durable bond, ensuring that the moulding stayed securely in place without the need for nails or screws.
I chose the FARLOV doors for their clean and classic design. These doors were installed at the standard height, perfectly complementing the custom trim and overall aesthetic of the bookcase.

MOULDING SIZE

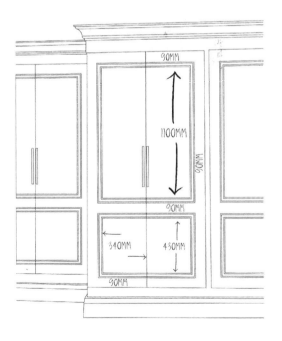

ÖVERSIDAN
LED wardrobe lighting
strp w sensor,
dimmable white, 96 cm

ARTICLE NO: 705.290.88

ARTICLE NO: 402.017.23

PAX 100CM
100x58x201 cm

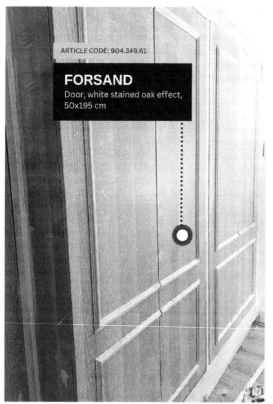

ARTICLE CODE: 904.349.61

FORSAND
Door, white stained oak effect,
50x195 cm

IKEA PAX HACK

THE DOOR OPENS

Check out my youtube channel
for more details.

IKEA PAX WARDROBE INFO

MEASURE YOUR ROOM:

- Measure the width, height, and depth of the space where you plan to install the wardrobe.
. Make sure you do this a few times, best to double-check everything.
- Note any architectural features such as windows, doors, or sloping ceilings that may affect the design.
- Consider Storage Needs:
- Determine what you need to store: clothes, shoes, accessories, etc.
- Think about specific storage solutions like hanging space, shelves, drawers, and shoe racks.

USE THE IKEA PAX PLANNER TOOL

- Visit the IKEA website and navigate to the Pax Planner tool.
- Create an account or log in to save your designs.
- Design Your Wardrobe:
- Input your room dimensions and select the type of wardrobe frames you want.
- Customize the interior by adding shelves, drawers, hanging rods, and other accessories.
- Experiment with different configurations to find the best layout for your needs.
- Choose from a variety of door styles, including hinged, sliding, or no doors.
- Consider the material and colour that will best match your room's decor.

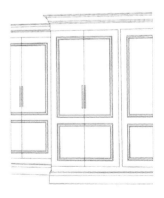

- Select handles or knobs that complement your chosen door style.
- I think about the finish and design that will enhance the overall look.
- Interior Accessories
- Explore additional accessories like pull-out trays, dividers, and lighting to enhance functionality.
- Determine a realistic budget for your project, including a buffer for unexpected expenses.

IKEA PAX WARDROBE INFO

CEILING HEIGHT 235CM

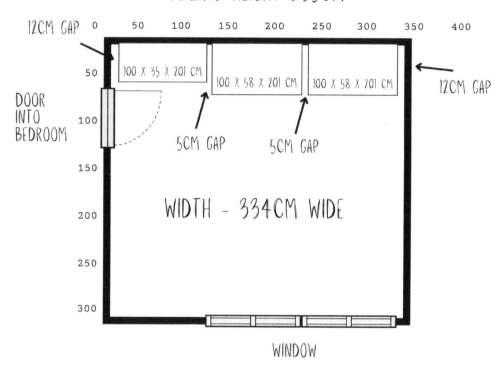

12CM GAP

DOOR INTO BEDROOM

100 X 35 X 201 CM

100 X 58 X 201 CM

100 X 58 X 201 CM

12CM GAP

5CM GAP

5CM GAP

WIDTH - 334CM WIDE

WINDOW

SHORT DEPTH OPTION

A tricky aspect of our Pax build was dealing with the bedroom door that seemed to be in the way! We wondered if opting for the short-depth Pax would mean losing valuable storage space. However, my husband actually prefers this setup. These shallower wardrobes cleverly feature a forward-facing hanging rail and compact drawers. We decided to enhance it further by adding shelves, which have provided my husband with incredibly useful storage for his books, golf equipment, document baskets, and shoes!

SHORT DEPTH OPTION

When building my PAX wardrobe, I created a sturdy foundation that allowed me to add skirting board along the front. I used C16 timber (the same material as the main frame) to construct the base. Here's a helpful tip: if you're keeping the existing skirting board behind the wardrobe, remember to factor this into your measurements when calculating the base depth. For the perfect fit, I made sure the base matched both the width of the gap and the exact depth of the PAX wardrobes. I also stacked two plants on top of each other (I have skirting over 16cm high)

BASE SIZE
C16 CLS TIMBER (L)330CM (W)56CM (ALLOWING FOR SKIRTING)

IKEA PAX WARDROBE INFO

I'm no fan of adding coving, but it really finishes this wardrobe off

THE RESULT

The end result was a beautifully organised and functional IKEA Pax wardrobe that met all our storage needs.
The adjustable shelves, drawers, and specialised accessories provided ample space for our clothes, shoes, and accessories, while the neutral colour palette and sleek design ensured the wardrobe complemented our bedroom decor perfectly. Choosing oak interiors significantly enhanced the aesthetic appeal of the wardrobes, imparting a refined, gentlemanly look. The rich, warm tones of oak added a touch of sophistication and elegance,

REFLECTIONS

Designing the interior of our IKEA Pax wardrobe was a rewarding experience. It allowed me to tailor the storage solutions to our specific needs and preferences, resulting in a space that was both practical and visually appealing. The flexibility of the Pax system means we can easily reconfigure the layout in the future as our storage needs change.
For a detailed walkthrough of this project, including tips and techniques, be sure to check out my YouTube video.
 I hope it inspires you to design your own customised IKEA Pax wardrobe and see the potential in creating a storage solution that works for you.

TOP TIPS

To design the interior of our IKEA Pax wardrobe, I made extensive use of the IKEA planning tool. I spent a significant amount of time carefully planning the layout, ensuring that every detail was perfect.
Initially, I purchased only the frame, doors, and hinges because the interior components I wanted were out of stock. Despite this, the planning tool allowed me to visualise and configure the ideal setup for our storage needs.

One of my top recommendations is the ÖVERSIDAN LED lights. These lights do an exceptional job of illuminating the interior, giving it a high-end look. I initially made the mistake of using battery-operated lights, which constantly ran out of power. Mains-powered lighting is definitely the way to go for a reliable and consistent light source.

Before

After

MY WARDROBE HACK HISTORY

this lasted 70 years

IKEA has given the PAX wardrobe a fresh new look, but guess what? It doesn't change a thing for my hacks or any other projects I've taken on. Why, you ask? It's all thanks to the solid wooden frame that anchors everything in place.

Recently, I dismantled a wardrobe in my bedroom that had been installed way back in the 1950s. It was held together by some of the biggest nails I've ever seen and made from the same material as these IKEA PAX wardrobes. It lasted over 70 years because of how securely it was fitted to the walls. That vintage wardrobe was the spark that ignited my inspiration for this modern makeover!

DESIGNING SHEET

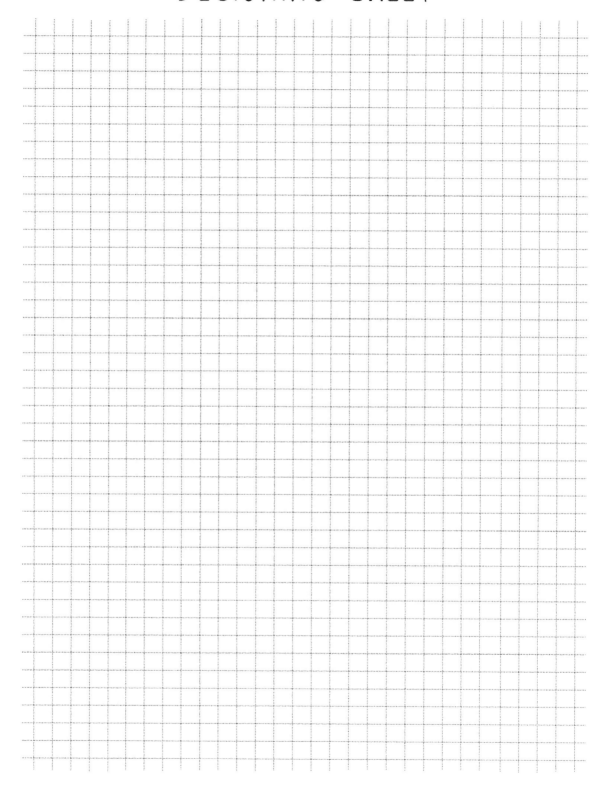

PROJECT PLANNER

Project Name

Start Date

End Date

Project Description

Must have features

Shopping list

Ideas & Notes

HALLWAY STORAGE HACK

FIRST TIME I'VE USED A TV STAND WITH A PAX

HALLWAY PAX HACK

HOW I BUILT THE IKEA HALLWAY PAX CUPBOARD

When organising our hallway, I knew we needed a practical and stylish solution that could handle the clutter of everyday life. After considering various options, I decided to build an IKEA Pax cupboard to maximise storage and enhance the aesthetic of our entryway. Our hallway was often cluttered with shoes, coats, bags, and other miscellaneous items. We needed a storage solution that could neatly organise these items and keep them out of sight.

I had the perfect space to build storage in our hall after we completed a kitchen extension, which involved blocking up the old kitchen door (thanks to our builders). Our hallway boasts the highest ceiling in the house, making it an ideal spot for taller Pax units. However, I envisioned incorporating a seating area into the unit, so I opted for a different approach.To achieve this, I used a LACK TV stand combined with a LAGKAPTEN oak-style worktop. This combination not only provided the necessary storage but also created a cozy and functional seating area, perfectly suited for our hallway.

The first step was to measure the hallway and plan the layout using IKEA's online Pax Planner tool. I opted for a combination of standard-height wardrobe units for coats, along with shelves and drawers for shoes and accessories. To create a functional base, I used a LACK TV stand. I secured the LACK TV stand in place first, ensuring it was stable and level. Then, I added a LAGKAPTEN worktop on top of the TV stand. I had to trim the worktop down to fit the space perfectly, positioning the cut side against the wall for a clean finish.

HALLWAY PAX HACK

To achieve a built-in look, I added MDF boards and custom trim around the edges of the Pax units. The trim not only enhanced the aesthetic appeal but also concealed any gaps, giving the units a polished, custom-built appearance. For the MDF boards, I took my measurements to B&Q and had them cut in-store. It's crucial to double-check the cuts while you're still at the store, as I've recently experienced issues with MDF being cut incorrectly. Ensuring accuracy at this stage saves a lot of hassle later on.

I applied a coat of primer to the MDF boards and trim. Once the primer dried, I painted the entire setup in a color that matched the hallway decor. I chose a soft white to keep the space looking bright and open. For those interested in the specifics of painting and sealing MDF, I have a dedicated YouTube video that covers the entire process in detail.

had removed a Pax unit from the entranceway, leaving me with two doors that I planned to reuse. However, I wasn't fond of the style of these doors, and they looked a bit odd in the new setup. Instead of buying a FÄRLÖV door, I decided to purchase another door in the same style that I wasn't keen on and customise it myself.

Next, I added coving to the top of the units for a refined, finished look. Some really nice gold handles were installed on the doors, adding a touch of elegance and sophistication. Inside, I added shelves and rails to maximise the storage functionality. With these final touches, the project was complete, resulting in a beautiful and functional hallway storage solution.

HALLWAY PAX HACK

HOW I CREATED IT

When it comes to maximizing storage and style in a small space, the hallway is often overlooked. However, with a bit of creativity and some DIY skills, even the narrowest of spaces can be transformed into a functional and aesthetically pleasing area. Here's how I turned my hallway into a masterpiece using IKEA Pax units.

THE INSPIRATION

Hallways are typically high-traffic areas that can quickly become cluttered with shoes, coats, and everyday items.

I wanted to create a storage solution that was not only practical but also visually appealing. The IKEA Pax system provided the perfect foundation for this project due to its versatility and customizable options.

MATERIALS NEEDED

- IKEA Pax wardrobe frames and doors
- LACK TV stand - White, 160x35x36 cm
- LAGKAPTEN Table top, white stained oak effect, 200x60 cm
- Additional shelves, rails, and accessories from the KOMPLEMENT system
- MDF boards or custom trim for a built-in look
- Wood filler
- Sandpaper
- Primer and paint
- Handles and hardware
- Tools: drill, saw, paintbrushes, and a level

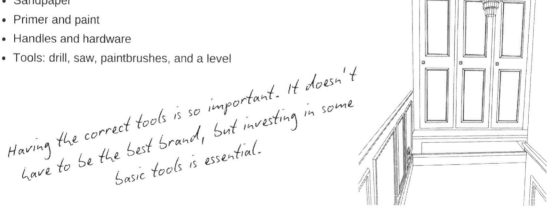

Having the correct tools is so important. It doesn't have to be the best brand, but investing in some basic tools is essential.

HALLWAY PAX HACK

STEP-BY-STEP PROCESS

Investing in a plug-in hand sander was a game changer

1. PLANNING AND DESIGNING

The first step was to measure the hallway and plan the layout using IKEA's online Pax Planner tool. I opted for a combination of standard-height wardrobe units for coats, along with shelves and drawers for shoes and accessories. To create a functional base, I used a LACK TV stand. I secured the frame at the back first, then the LACK TV stand, ensuring it was stable and level. Then, I added a LAGKAPTEN worktop on top of the TV stand. I had to trim the worktop down to fit the space perfectly, positioning the cut side against the wall for a clean finish. I made a small wooden frame behind the LACK to extend the base.

2. ASSEMBLY

Next, I assembled the Pax units according to IKEA's instructions. This step was straightforward but required careful alignment to ensure a seamless fit. I made sure to leave enough space between the units and the ceiling for custom trim.

3. CUSTOMISATION WITH TRIM

To achieve a built-in look, I added MDF boards and custom trim around the edges of the Pax units. This step involved precise measurements and cuts to ensure a snug fit. The trim not only enhanced the aesthetic appeal but also concealed any gaps, giving the units a polished, custom-built appearance.

4. FILLING AND SANDING

I filled any gaps and screw holes with wood filler and sanded the entire surface for a smooth finish. This preparation is key to achieving a professional look when painting.

Investing in a plug in hand sander was a game changer

5. PRIMING AND PAINTING

I applied a coat of primer to the MDF boards and trim. Once the primer dried, I painted the entire setup in a colour that matched the hallway decor. I chose a soft white to keep the space looking bright and open. For those interested in the specifics of painting and sealing MDF, I have a dedicated YouTube video that covers the entire process in detail.

6. ADDING HARDWARE

To personalise the units, I selected elegant handles and hardware that complemented the overall design. These small details added a touch of sophistication and tied the look together.

7. SECURING THE UNITS

For safety and stability, I secured the Pax units to the wall using brackets. This step is crucial, especially in high-traffic areas like hallways, to prevent the units from tipping over.

IKEA HALLWAY PAX INFO

HOW TO DESIGN YOUR PAX

MEASURE YOUR ROOM:

- Measure the width, height, and depth of the space where you plan to install the pax units.
- Note any architectural features such as windows, doors, or sloping ceilings that may affect the design.
- Consider Storage Needs:
- Determine what you need to store: coats, shoes, accessories, etc.
- Think about specific storage solutions like hanging space, shelves, drawers, and shoe racks.

USE THE IKEA PAX PLANNER TOOL:

- Visit the IKEA website and navigate to the Pax Planner tool.
- Create an account or log in to save your designs.
- Input your room dimensions and select the type of wardrobe frames you want.
- Customize the interior by adding shelves, drawers, hanging rods, and other accessories.
- Experiment with different configurations to find the best layout for your needs.
- Choose from a variety of door styles, including hinged, sliding, or no doors.
- Consider the material and colour that will best match your room's decor.
- Select handles or knobs that complement your chosen door style.
- I think about the finish and design that will enhance the overall look.
- Interior Accessories
- Explore additional accessories like pull-out trays, dividers, and lighting to enhance functionality.
- Determine a realistic budget for your project, including a buffer for unexpected expenses.

PAX

Wardrobe frame, white stained oak effect, 50x58x201 cm

ARTICLE NO: 202.017.24

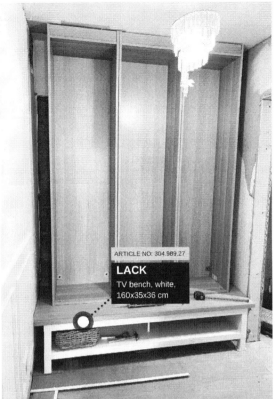

ARTICLE NO: 304.989.27

LACK

TV bench, white, 160x35x36 cm

18MM MDF

Cut from a large sheet in B&Q

IKEA PAX HACK

OAK INTERIOR

Check out my youtube channel for more details.

IKEA HALLWAY PAX INFO

CEILING HEIGHT 235CM

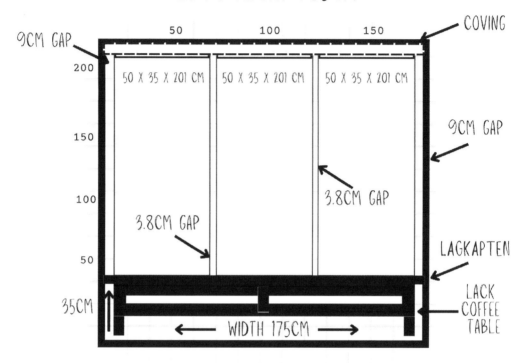

9CM GAP

COVING

50   100   150

200

50 X 35 X 201 CM   50 X 35 X 201 CM   50 X 35 X 201 CM

150

9CM GAP

100

3.8CM GAP

3.8CM GAP

50

LAGKAPTEN

35CM

LACK COFFEE TABLE

WIDTH 175CM

I made a basic frame behind the LACK. I made it fit the area

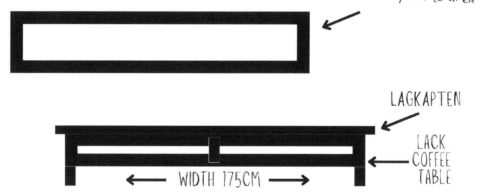

LAGKAPTEN

LACK COFFEE TABLE

WIDTH 175CM

HALLWAY PAX HACK

THE RESULT

The transformation was remarkable. What was once a cluttered and uninspiring hallway became a streamlined, functional, and beautiful space. The Pax units provided ample storage for coats, shoes, and accessories, while the custom trim and paint gave the setup a high-end, bespoke look.

TIPS AND TRICKS

- Plan Thoroughly: Use IKEA's Pax Planner tool to visualise the design and ensure all components fit your space.
- Measure Carefully: Precision is vital when adding custom trim and MDF boards.
- Invest in Quality Paint: High-quality paint will provide a smooth and durable finish, essential for high-traffic areas.
- Personalise with Hardware: Unique handles and hardware can elevate the overall design and add a personal touch.

CONCLUSION

Building my hallway Pax IKEA hack was an incredibly rewarding project that transformed a mundane space into something special. The combination of practicality and style has made the hallway one of my favourite areas in the house. I hope my experience inspires you to tackle your own DIY projects and unlock the potential of every space in your home. Happy hacking!

I've lost count of how many times I've been asked about this light - a bargain £19.99 Ebay find.

DESIGNING SHEET

PROJECT PLANNER

Project Name

Start Date

End Date

Project Description

Must have features

Shopping list

Ideas & Notes

IKEA SECRET BAR HACK

SECRET BAR HACK

The stunning tree wallpaper I used on this dresser was a dupe from B&Q at only £20 a roll

HOW I CREATED THIS SECRET BAR.

This hack began way back in 2021. Originally, we planned to include a wine room in our extension. However, for various reasons, that plan fell through. Determined to create a stylish solution, I decided to build something in our main kitchen. Needing more storage, I figured using these storage units on the bottom and creating a multifunctional unit with a pull-out bar would be the best idea.

I spent quite some time browsing Facebook and eBay for dressers, sideboards, and chests of drawers, but I never found anything I liked. Then, after seeing these cabinets used in hacks on Instagram, I decided to use them to create this secret bar.

Now, I'm not much of a drinker, but I've always admired the glamorous setups of bars and wine rooms and how they look in a home. With my husband very keen on having a bar at home, I set to work on creating this secret bar.

Let me show you how I transformed this dresser by day into a sparkling bar by night!

LOMMARP
Cabinet, light beige,
102x101 cm

ARTICLE NO: 104.369.97

ARTICLE NO: 302.638.44

BILLY
Bookcase, white,
80x28x106 cm

ARTICLE CODE: 003.356.25

EKBACKEN
Worktop, white marble
effect/laminate, 246x2.8 cm

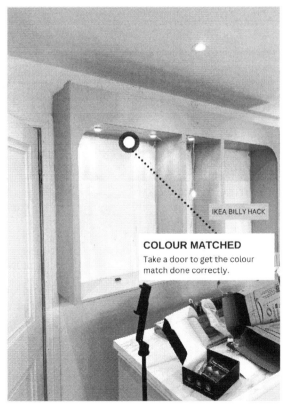

IKEA BILLY HACK

COLOUR MATCHED
Take a door to get the colour
match done correctly.

SECRET BAR HACK INFO

CEILING HEIGHT 235CM

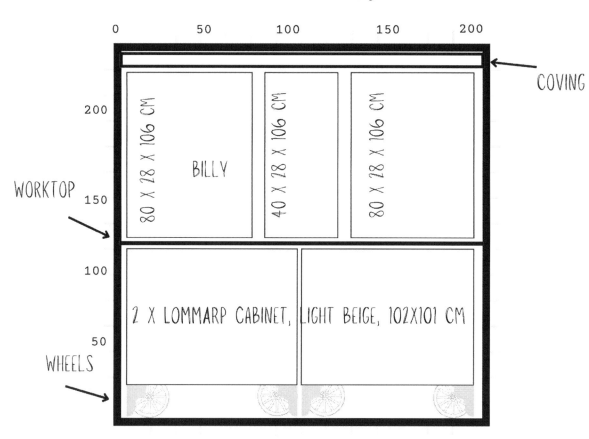

COVING

WORKTOP

WHEELS

80 X 28 X 106 CM

BILLY

40 X 28 X 106 CM

80 X 28 X 106 CM

2 X LOMMARP CABINET, LIGHT BEIGE, 102X101 CM

WIDTH 210CM

SECRET BAR HACK

HOW TO DESIGN YOUR PAX

Here's an overview of the process and key steps involved:

MATERIALS NEEDED:

- 3 x IKEA BILLY bookcases
- 2 x LOMMARP units
- Fake marble worktop
- Industrial wheels
- Self-adhesive wallpaper
- LED strip lights
- Screws, nails, and basic tools

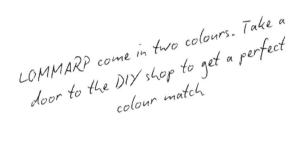

LOMMARP come in two colours. Take a door to the DIY shop to get a perfect colour match

ASSEMBLING THE BOOKCASES:

I kicked off the project by assembling the two IKEA BILLY bookcases, carefully following the provided instructions. Ensuring they were securely fastened to the wall was crucial, as they needed to hover just above the pull-out base unit. For added stability, I highly recommend using kitchen wall cabinet fixings. Next, I built the two LOMMARP units and fixed them together. To make them sit flush next to each other, I had to trim down one side. While this step isn't necessary for everyone, my tight space required this adjustment.

ADDING MOBILITY:

To make the bar easily movable, I attached industrial 4 wheels to the bottom of each bookcase, 8 in total. This step involves measuring and securing the wheels with screws, ensuring stability and ease of movement.

CUSTOMISING THE WORKTOP:

I then cut a fake marble worktop to perfectly fit across the top of the bookcases I bought from IKEA. After trimming down one side, I adhered the supplied strip for a seamless finish. This worktop not only offers a sleek and modern surface but also ties together the overall aesthetic of the bar. Opting for faux marble was a smart choice, as it is both lightweight and stylish.

ENHANCING WITH GLASS & LIGHTING:

IKEA now offers glass shelves for the BILLY bookcase, and they were perfect for creating this secret bar. Once I installed them, I added LED strip lights along the inner edges of the bookcases. By directing the lights towards the back, I achieved a beautiful, warm glow that enhanced the inviting ambiance of the bar.

SECRET BAR HACK

DECORATING THE BACK:

For the finishing touches, I added coving along the top, pine strips to cover the Billy frame, and applied wallpaper to the back of the LOMMARP bookcases. I also cut out a section from the back of the LOMMARP, providing easy access to the bottles in the cabinet when the bar is pulled out. To ensure a cohesive look, I painted everything in a colour that matched the LOMMARP cabinets. I brought an inside shelf to the DIY store for a colour match, but in hindsight, taking a door would have been better as the color turned out slightly darker. Finally, I decorated the back of the LOMMARP bookcases with self-adhesive wallpaper, which was super easy to apply.

THE FINAL RESULT:

The end result is a stunning secret bar that blends seamlessly with the rest of the room. I absolutely love how this project turned out, as the bar is both functional and stylish. Its hidden nature, appearing as a regular dresser during the day, adds a definite wow factor. It has now become a standard ritual to pull out the bar whenever guests come over, and it always garners an enthusiastic response!

CONCLUSION:

This project not only showcases how easy it is to create something beautiful with IKEA pieces, but it also serves as an inspiration for others to reimagine their own spaces. I hope this encourages you to get creative and transform your home in ways you never thought possible!

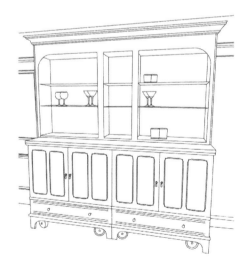

DESIGNING SHEET

PROJECT PLANNER

Project Name

Start Date

End Date

Project Description

Must have features

Shopping list

Ideas & Notes

SHOE STORAGE HACK

SUPER EASY HACK!

HALL SHOE RACK

MY IKEA STALL HALLWAY SHOE HACK

Transforming a mundane piece of furniture into something stylish and functional is one of the most satisfying aspects of DIY projects.

My IKEA STALL hallway shoe hack is a perfect example of how a little creativity and effort can turn a simple shoe rack into a chic and practical addition to your home. With the limited width of our entrance hall, I always knew I'd opt for a thin shoe rack. However, I wasn't fond of the cut-out shelf detail on the STALL IKEA shoe cupboards. Despite this, they are ideal for small spaces, offering just enough width to accommodate a small lamp, a vase of flowers, or a car key dish on top.

HALL SHOE RACK

MATERIALS NEEDED

- IKEA STALL shoe rack
- Paint or wallpaper (optional, for customisation)
- Decorative handles or knobs
- LED strip lights (optional, for added flair)
- No more nails/glue
- Basic tools: screwdriver, tape measure, etc.

Adding LED lights around the outside would give this a great look

EASY WAYS TO HACK THE STALL SHOE RACK:

CUSTOMISE THE EXTERIOR:

- To give the shoe rack a unique look, consider painting it in a colour that matches your décor or applying wallpaper to the front panels. This step allows you to personalise the shoe rack to fit seamlessly into your space. I just decided to paint it.

ADD EXTRA FEATURES:

- I added a thicker top to the top, and I also individually added half wooden balls to add some extra detail. Pine mouldings are a great way to add a bespoke look to the STALL shoe rack. I also added a thin piece of MDF to the front to cover the handle gap.

ADD DECORATIVE HANDLES:

- Replace the standard handles with decorative knobs or handles to enhance the aesthetic appeal of the shoe rack. Choose knobs that complement the overall design and colour scheme you've chosen.

INSTALL LED STRIP LIGHTS (OPTIONAL):

- For a touch of modernity and functionality, add LED strip lights along the inner edges of the shelves. This not only illuminates the shoe rack but also adds a stylish glow, making it easier to find your shoes in low light.

FINAL TOUCHES:

- Add any final decorative touches, such as small plants, picture frames, or other accessories that will complement the shoe rack and surrounding area.

DESIGNING MY HALL SHOE RACK

STALL SHOE CABINET WITH 4 COMPARTMENTS, WHITE, 96X17X90 CM

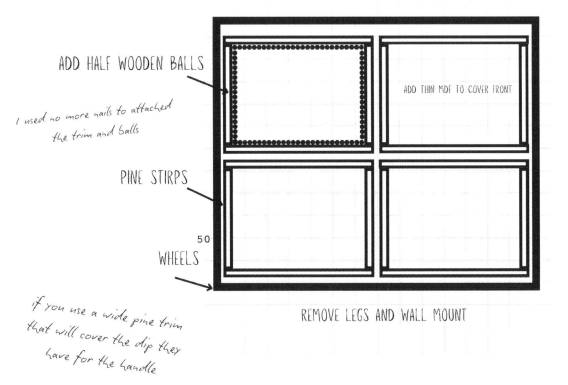

ADD HALF WOODEN BALLS

I used no more nails to attached the trim and balls

ADD THIN MDF TO COVER FRONT

PINE STIRPS

50

WHEELS

if you use a wide pine trim that will cover the dip they have for the handle

REMOVE LEGS AND WALL MOUNT

WHY THIS HACK WORKS:

SPACE-SAVING DESIGN:

The STALL shoe rack is designed to fit into narrow spaces, making it perfect for entryways or small closets.

CUSTOMISATION:

By painting, adding wallpaper, or incorporating pine mouldings and half wooden balls, you can tailor the shoe rack to match your personal style and home décor. You can buy a ball-style moulding but its really expensive. The individual half balls were much cheaper.

FUNCTIONALITY:

The addition of LED lights, a thicker top panel, and decorative handles not only enhances the look but also improves usability.

STÄLL
Shoe cabinet with 4 compartments, white, 96x17x90 cm

ARTICLE NO: 605.302.66

MDF TOP
18mm MDF

WOODEN 1/2 BALLS
These are 10mm. I added these using No more nails.

IKEA PAX HACK

REMOVED THE LEGS
I took them off so I had the floating look.

HALL SHOE RACK

TOP TIPS FOR THE IKEA STALL SHOE RACK HACK:

- Plan Ahead: Sketch out your design and gather all necessary materials before starting the project.
- Customisation: Use paint or wallpaper to match the shoe rack with your home décor.
- Add Details: Half wooden balls and pine mouldings can significantly enhance the look of the shoe rack.
- Thicker Top: Replacing the original top with a thicker panel adds a high-end feel.
- Functional Enhancements: Consider adding LED strip lights for both style and practicality.
- Secure Fixings: Ensure all parts are securely fastened to avoid any instability.
- Decorative Handles: Choose decorative knobs or handles to elevate the overall aesthetic.

WHAT I LEARNED DOING THIS HACK:

- Attention to Detail: Small decorative elements like half wooden balls can make a big difference.
- Patience is Key: Taking your time to customise and build the unit properly pays off.
- Versatility of IKEA Furniture: With a bit of creativity, you can transform basic IKEA pieces into bespoke furniture.
- Importance of Planning: Proper planning and preparation can save time and prevent mistakes.

HOW WELL IT TURNED OUT:

- Stunning Transformation: The STALL shoe rack turned into a chic and functional piece of furniture.
- Positive Feedback: The final product received a lot of positive feedback for its stylish and practical design.
- Enhanced Space: The shoe rack not only provided storage but also added a decorative element to the room.
- Satisfying Project: Completing the hack was incredibly satisfying and showcased the potential of DIY projects.

CONCLUSION

Building my hallway STALL IKEA hack was an incredibly rewarding project that transformed a mundane space into something special. The combination of practicality and style has made the hallway one of my favourite areas in the house. I hope my experience inspires you to tackle your own DIY projects and unlock the potential of every space in your home. Happy hacking!

NOTES

Use these notes pages to critique my hacks. Note down any changes you'd make and how you would adapt them to fit into your home. I make notes all the time—my mind never really switches off, so I've trained myself to write everything down!

PROJECT PLANNER

Project Name

Start Date

End Date

Project Description

Must have features

Shopping list

Ideas & Notes

HANDMADE WITH LOVE

PLANNING YOUR HACK

PLANNING YOUR HACK

PLANNING A DIY HACK: A STEP-BY-STEP GUIDE

Embarking on a DIY project can be both exciting and daunting. The key to a successful endeavour lies in thorough planning and preparation. Here's a detailed guide to help you plan your DIY hack, from research to budgeting.

RESEARCH AND INFORMATION

The first step in planning any DIY project is gathering information. Understanding the scope, materials, and techniques involved is crucial for a successful outcome. Here's where to find the information you need:

- **Online Resources:** Websites like Pinterest, YouTube, and DIY blogs are goldmines for inspiration and tutorials. Channels like my YouTube offer step-by-step guides and creative ideas.

- **Books and Magazines:** There are numerous books and magazines dedicated to DIY projects.

- **Forums and Communities:** Online communities on Facebook and DIY forums can be great places to ask questions, share ideas, and learn from others' experiences.

- **Workshops and Classes:** Local home improvement stores often offer workshops and classes on various DIY topics. Participating in these can provide hands-on experience and expert advice.

WHAT'S YOUR STYLE?

Defining your style is essential for creating a cohesive and aesthetically pleasing project. Consider the following elements:

- **Materials:** Choose materials that align with your style. For a rustic look, opt for reclaimed wood or metal. For a modern feel, consider sleek surfaces like glass and polished metals.
- **Colours:** Select a colour palette that complements your existing decor. Neutral tones provide a timeless look, while bold colours can make a statement.
- **Finish:** The finish you choose can dramatically affect the final appearance. Matte finishes offer a subtle, understated look, while glossy finishes add a touch of glamour.
- **Inspiration Boards:** Create an inspiration board using platforms like Pinterest to visualise your style. Collect images, colour swatches, and material samples to guide your design decisions.

PLANNING YOUR HACK

WHAT YOU NEED

Creating a comprehensive list of materials and tools is crucial for staying organised and ensuring you have everything you need. Here's how to do it:

- **List Everything:** Write down every item you'll need, from major materials like wood and paint to smaller items like screws and sandpaper.
- **Categorise:** Organise your list into categories such as materials, tools, and hardware. This makes it easier to keep track of what you have and what you still need to acquire.
- **Research Suppliers:** Use the internet to find suppliers for your materials. Websites like Amazon, Home Depot, B&Q and specialised DIY stores offer a wide range of options. Compare prices and read reviews to ensure you're getting quality products.
- **Local Stores:** Don't overlook local suppliers and thrift stores. They can be great sources for unique materials and often offer competitive prices.

I spend hours scribbling down designs in my DIY notebook. I like to keep them all together.

HOW TO DRAW YOUR PLAN

Planning your project on paper helps visualise the final product and identify potential issues before you start. Here's how to draw your plan:

- **Floor Plan:** If your project involves a room or large space, start with a floor plan. Measure the area accurately and draw it to scale. Include windows, doors, and other architectural features.
- **Design Sketches:** Create detailed sketches of your design. Include measurements, materials, and notes on construction techniques. This helps you visualise the project and serves as a reference during construction.
- **Design Software:** Consider using design software like SketchUp or RoomSketcher for more complex projects. These tools allow you to create 3D models and detailed plans.
- **My Design Paper:** Use graph paper or "My Design Paper" to draw precise, scaled drawings. This helps ensure accuracy and provides a clear blueprint to follow.

HACK PROJECT PLANNER

HERE ARE THE TOP 4 ESSENTIALS WHEN PLANNING AN IKEA HACK

Vision and Creativity:
Have a clear idea of what you want to achieve with the hack. This involves visualising the final product and thinking creatively about how you can transform standard IKEA products into something unique and functional.

Tools and Materials:
Gather all necessary tools and materials before starting your project. This might include basic tools like a drill, screwdriver, and measuring tape, as well as any additional materials such as paint, fabric, or hardware that will help customise your furniture.

Measurements and Planning:
Accurately measure the space where the IKEA hack will be placed and ensure that the dimensions of the furniture pieces fit perfectly. Plan the steps needed to execute the hack successfully, including any modifications you'll need to make to the original pieces.

Safety and Durability:
Consider the safety and durability of the final product. Make sure that any structural changes do not compromise the stability of the furniture. Use quality materials and proper techniques to ensure that the finished piece is safe and long-lasting.

Before

After

PLANNING YOUR HACK

SET YOUR BUDGET

Budgeting is an essential part of planning any DIY project. Here's how to price up your project and shop around for the best deals:

- **Estimate Costs:** Start by estimating the cost of materials, tools, and any additional expenses. Use your comprehensive list of items to create a detailed budget.
- **Research Prices:** Look up prices for each item on your list. Compare prices from different suppliers to find the best deals. Websites like PriceGrabber and Google Shopping can help with price comparisons.
- **Include a Contingency:** Add a contingency (usually 10-20% of the total budget) to account for unexpected expenses. This ensures you're not caught off guard by unforeseen costs.
- **Shop Around:** Don't settle for the first price you find. Shop around both online and in-store to ensure you're getting the best value for your money.
- **Track Your Spending:** Keep track of all your expenses throughout the project. This helps you stay within budget and adjust if necessary.

CONCLUSION

Planning a DIY hack requires careful research, a clear vision of your style, thorough preparation, and meticulous budgeting. By following these steps, you'll be well-equipped to tackle your project with confidence and creativity. Happy hacking!

When using MDF I like to buy the biggest sheets and get the DIY store to cut down. This can save you money over buying smaller pieces. Use the planner paper to plot out cuts on large sheets!

HOW MUCH IS IT GOING TO COST YOU?

(OCTOBER 2024)

Here's a breakdown of potential costs for building an IKEA PAX wardrobe in the UK, with prices in pounds sterling. The total cost will depend on your specific configuration and additional features, so this serves as a general guide:

WARDROBE FRAMES

PAX Frames: Available in different sizes and finishes. Prices vary based on size:

Small (50x58x201 cm): £50 - £70 each
Medium (75x58x201 cm): £70 - £90 each
Large (100x58x201 cm): £90 - £130 each

DOORS

Hinged Doors: Range from £40 to £80 per door, depending on the style.
Sliding Doors: Range from £80 to £250 per pair, depending on the design and material.

INTERIOR ORGANIZATION

Shelves: £8 to £25 each, depending on material and size.
Drawers: £12 to £35 each, with options for soft-close mechanisms.
Clothes Rails: Approximately £8 each.
Pull-out Trays/Baskets: £12 to £25 each.
Shoe Racks: Around £15 each.

ACCESSORIES

Lighting: Integrated LED lighting options can range from £12 to £40.
Dividers and Organizers: £4 to £18 each, depending on size and material.
Mirrors: Add-on mirrors start at £12.

ASSEMBLY COSTS (OPTIONAL)

Assembly Service: If you choose IKEA's assembly service, it might add around £40 to £120 to the total cost, depending on the complexity and size of the wardrobe.

DELIVERY COSTS (OPTIONAL)

Delivery: Costs can vary based on location and order size, typically starting at £20

ESTIMATED TOTAL COST

A basic PAX wardrobe with hinged doors and a few interior fittings might cost around £250 to £400. A more complex wardrobe with sliding doors, custom interiors, and additional features could range from £600 to £1,000 or more.

These are approximate costs, and actual prices might vary based on your location and specific choices. It's advisable to visit the IKEA website or your local store for the most accurate pricing and availability.

BUY SECOND HAND

Scoring amazing IKEA furniture deals on platforms like Facebook Marketplace is a savvy way to keep your home chic and functional without breaking the bank. Imagine my thrill when I snagged an IKEA Billy bookcase from a neighbor down the street for just £10! You might have to embark on a little road trip, but often, people are practically giving away Billy bookcases for free. And if the color isn't quite your style, why not unleash your creativity and give them a fresh coat of paint?

UPCYCLING

HOW TO MEASURE THE SPACE

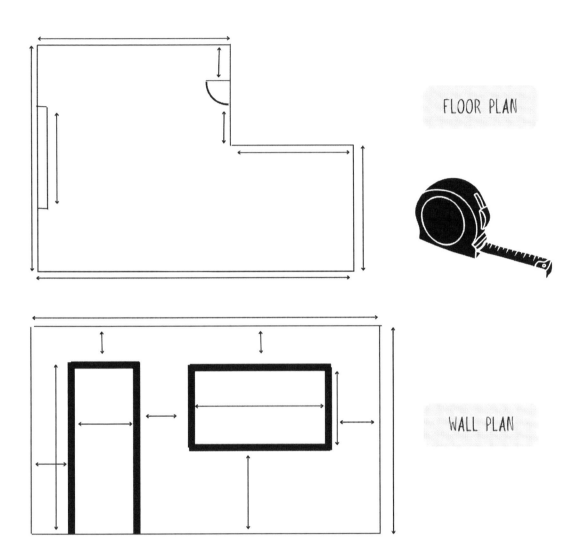

FLOOR PLAN

WALL PLAN

MY TOP TIPS

- Buy a good tape measure & ruler.
- Walls are usually not straight. I always recommend measuring on the top, middle, and bottom.
- Make a note of any sockets and switches.
- Are any items moving? Like radiators?
- Measure all doors
- Measure all the windows

THINGS TO REMEMBER

- Make a note of what the walls are made of, plasterboard? Solid wall?
- Is the floor wooden or concrete?
- Are you removing coving? If you take it off it might need plastering over.
- Are you changing the ceiling?
- Are you replacing doors or windows?
- Are you replacing skirting boards?

SHOPPING LIST

Budgeting is an essential part of planning any DIY project. Here's how to price up your project and shop around for the best deals:

Creating a shopping list for a DIY hack is crucial to ensure you have all the necessary materials and tools before starting your project. A well-organised list helps streamline the process, prevents multiple trips to the store, and keeps your project on track.

DIY HACK SHOPPING LIST

When planning your DIY hack, it's essential to gather all the materials and tools you'll need. Here's a detailed shopping list template to help you stay organised and prepared:

PROJECT OVERVIEW

Project Name:
- Example: "Custom Built-In Bookshelf"

Project Description:
- Example: "Transform a plain wall into a custom built-in bookshelf using MDF boards, trim, and paint."

MATERIALS

Primary Materials:
- MDF boards (specify dimensions and quantity)
- Trim (specify type and length)
- Paint (specify color and type)
- Primer, Caulk, Wood filler

Hardware:
- Screws (specify size and quantity)
- Nails (specify size and quantity)
- Brackets (if needed for stability)
- Handles or knobs (if applicable)

Finishing Supplies:
- Sandpaper (various grits)
- Paintbrushes and rollers, Painter's tape, Drop cloths

SHOPPING LIST

TOOLS

Essential Tools:
- Drill and drill bits
- Saw (circular saw, jigsaw, or handsaw depending on the cuts needed)
- Measuring tape
- Level
- Screwdrivers
- Hammer
- Putty knife

Additional Tools:
- Miter box (for cutting trim)
- Sander (optional but recommended for a smoother finish)
- Caulking gun

MISCELLANEOUS

Additional Items:
- Wood glue
- Cleaning supplies (rags, cleaning solution)
- Storage containers for small hardware

NOTES AND TIPS

Project-Specific Tips:
- Measure your space twice before purchasing materials to ensure accuracy.
- Check for any special sales or discounts at your local or online stores.
- Consider buying a little extra material to account for any mistakes or adjustments.

SHOPPING
LIST

IKEA PAX WARDROBE HACK

1. Pax wardrobe 100 x 2
2. Pax wardrobe 50 x 1
3. MDF - 18mm sheet
4. No-more nail
5. Pack of screws
6. Drill bit
7. 8 x wood 2.4m

I LOVE SQUARED PAPER

Writing on blank paper is a timeless method for capturing ideas, whether they arrive as a sudden spark of inspiration or a well-thought-out concept. The simplicity and freedom of blank paper make it an ideal canvas for creativity. Without the constraints of lines or grids, individuals can express thoughts in any form—be it doodles, mind maps, sketches, or notes. This flexibility encourages free thinking and allows ideas to flow naturally, making it easier to brainstorm and refine concepts.

In the realm of design, squared paper, like graph paper, brings its own set of unique benefits. The grid pattern acts as a trusty guide, helping you maintain perfect proportions and alignment. This is especially handy when you're sketching layouts, creating technical drawings, or planning intricate patterns. The squares serve as a reliable reference for scale and distance, making it easier to visualise how elements relate to one another spatially. Personally, I find square paper indispensable, and I've included a few pages at the back of this book for you to unleash your creativity and sketch out some ideas.

Measuring accurately and jotting things down on square paper is my go-to method for ensuring everything aligns perfectly.

DESIGNERS OFTEN USE SQUARED PAPER FOR:

Architectural Sketches: The grid helps in maintaining scale and proportion, essential for architectural planning.

Graphic Design Layouts: This allows for precise alignment of elements, ensuring a clean and professional look.

Technical Illustrations: Engineers and designers can benefit from the accuracy that squared paper provides for technical drawings.

Both blank and squared paper have their places in the creative process, each offering distinct advantages that can cater to different stages of ideation and design development. Whether it's the freeform nature of blank paper or the structured guidance of squared paper, the key is to choose the right tool to unlock your creativity and bring your ideas to life.

DESIGNING SHEET

...est in ruler! I've got a basic pencil case with drawing pens and pencils

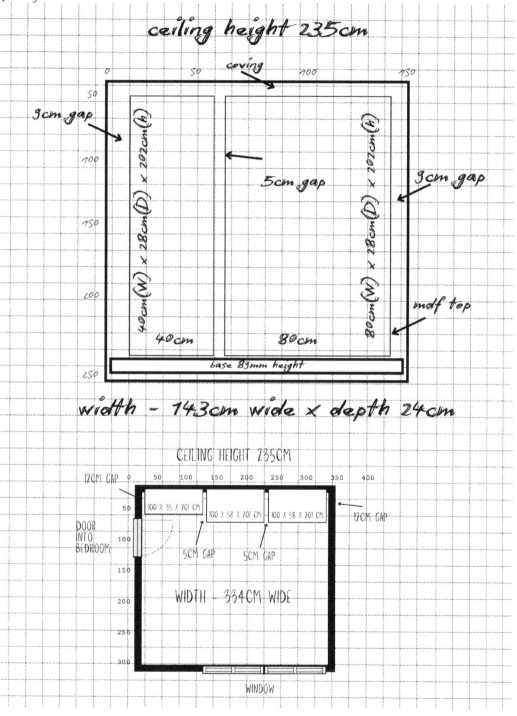

ceiling height 235cm

0   50   coving   100   150

50

9cm gap

40cm(W) x 28cm(D) x 202cm(h)

100

5cm gap

9cm gap

150

200

80cm(W) x 28cm(D) x 202cm(h)

mdf top

40cm   80cm

250   base 89mm height

width - 143cm wide x depth 24cm

CEILING HEIGHT 235CM

12CM GAP 0   50   100   150   200   250   300   350   400

50   100 X 35 X 201 CM   100 X 58 X 201 CM   100 X 58 X 201 CM   12CM GAP

DOOR
INTO   100
BEDROOM
          5CM GAP   5CM GAP
150

200   WIDTH - 334CM WIDE

250

300

WINDOW

IDEAS & SCRIBBLES

HALLWAY STORAGE PAX BUILD

Colour match Dulux

Favorite Colour

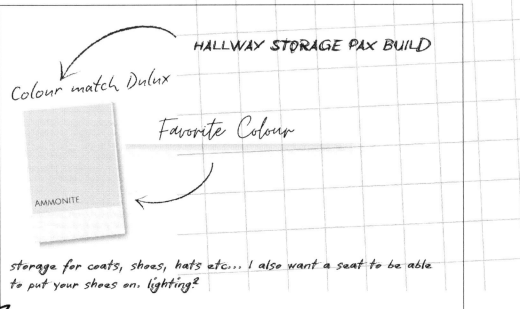

AMMONITE

storage for coats, shoes, hats etc... I also want a seat to be able
to put your shoes on. lighting?

I couldn't be happier with how this hallway storage transformation turned out! What was once a rather dingy space has now blossomed into a much-needed cupboard. The best part? You can customize the interior to your heart's content. I highly recommend trying out the IKEA Pax design tool—it's fantastic for visualising exactly what you can fit inside these units.

PAINTING YOUR HACKS

PAINTING YOUR HACKS

THE ART OF TRANSFORMING IKEA FURNITURE:

TIPS AND TECHNIQUES FOR PAINTING AND PREPPING

Transforming IKEA furniture into a unique and personal masterpiece is a trend that has swept through the DIY community like a creative whirlwind. Whether you're looking to add a pop of color to your living room or give your office a sophisticated touch, transforming IKEA pieces can be as simple or intricate as your imagination allows. One of the most effective methods of personalizing these pieces is through painting. This guide will walk you through the essential practices for prepping and painting your IKEA furniture, ensuring a professional and enduring finish. This is the tried-and-true method I've used on my own hacks included in this book.

CHOOSING THE RIGHT PIECE

Before plunging into the painting process, it's crucial to select the right piece of IKEA furniture. Consider the material and finish of the item. Solid wood pieces are ideal since they hold paint exceptionally well, but with the proper preparation, laminate surfaces can also be beautifully transformed. Additionally, think about how frequently the piece will be used, as this will influence your prep and paint choices.

GATHERING YOUR SUPPLIES

To ensure a smooth painting process, gather the following supplies:

- Sandpaper (medium and fine grit)
- Primer suitable for the furniture material
- High-quality paint (chalk paint will work well)
- Paintbrushes and rollers
- Drop cloth or old newspapers
- Painter's tape
- A clean cloth
- Screwdriver (for disassembling furniture if necessary)

DISASSEMBLING AND CLEANING

Start by disassembling the furniture as much as possible. This facilitates easier access to all surfaces, ensuring a more thorough paint job. Next, clean the surfaces with a damp cloth to eliminate any dust, dirt, or grease. For laminate surfaces, using a gentle degreaser can be beneficial. Personally, I often paint my pieces when they are fully assembled, but this really depends on the specific project and usage.

SANDING THE SURFACES

Sanding is often hailed as a crucial step, especially for laminate surfaces. I recommend sanding if you're working on items like coffee tables or dining tables that will endure significant use and risk of chipping. Use medium-grit sandpaper to lightly sand all surfaces you plan to paint. This creates a texture that helps the primer adhere more effectively. Ensure you wipe away all dust with a clean cloth or tack cloth. In my personal experience, I sometimes skip sanding, such as with my IKEA doors, as I handle them with care. Two years in, they have remained chip-free, but for guaranteed longevity, a light sanding is advisable.

PRIMING

Applying a primer is essential for both wood and laminate surfaces. Choose a primer that complements the furniture material. A high-adhesion primer is recommended for laminate surfaces to prevent peeling. Apply a thin, even coat of primer with a brush or roller and let it dry completely, following the manufacturer's instructions. For large areas, I use a small roller, and for detailed pine moldings, a brush works best.

PAINTING YOUR HACKS

PAINTING TECHNIQUES

- Choosing the Paint: Latex paint is durable and easy to clean, making it an excellent choice for furniture. Chalk paint offers a matte finish and is forgiving for beginners. I am particularly fond of Dulux brilliant white wood & metal paint, which I've used on all my white hacks.
- Application: Use a quality brush for edges and detailed areas. Avoid the rounded brushes commonly available, as they can cause blisters. For flat surfaces, a foam roller can provide a smooth finish. Apply thin, even coats, allowing each layer to dry as per the paint manufacturer's instructions before applying the next. Patience is key—there's no need to rush!
- Multiple Coats: For optimal results, apply at least two coats of paint, ensuring even coverage and vibrant color. My Pax wardrobes required three coats, and four coats were necessary for the oak doors. To make the process more enjoyable, I often have something playing on Netflix in the background.

FINISHING TOUCHES

Once the final coat of paint has dried, consider applying a clear protective finish, especially for pieces that will experience heavy use. A polyurethane topcoat can add durability and make the surface easier to clean. Allow the finish to cure fully according to the product instructions. While I didn't add this to my IKEA Pax hacks, I did apply it to the oak hack featured on my YouTube channel, as it was a bedside table and I wanted to protect the top.

REASSEMBLING AND STYLING

If you've dismantled your IKEA furniture, only reassemble it after the paint has fully dried and cured. Use painter's tape to add patterns or designs for additional flair before reassembling if desired. Finally, accessorize your piece with new hardware or other decorative elements to enhance its new look. I always attach my moldings and trims before priming and painting.

PAINTING YOUR HACKS

IN CONCLUSION

The art of transforming IKEA furniture through painting is not only accessible but also an incredibly rewarding endeavor. This project allows individuals to breathe new life into their furniture pieces, turning them into personalised and stylish expressions of their unique taste. The process begins with the careful selection of the right piece, ensuring it complements the intended design and fits well within your space.

Once the perfect piece is chosen, thorough preparation is key to achieving a flawless finish. This involves cleaning the surfaces meticulously, sanding them to create the ideal texture for paint adhesion, and priming to ensure long-lasting results. These preparatory steps are crucial, as they set the foundation for the painting process and ultimately determine the quality and durability of the final product.

The painting stage itself is where creativity truly shines. By applying paint with care and attention to detail, you can craft a piece that not only meets your aesthetic goals but also serves as a conversation starter in your home. Whether opting for bold, vibrant colors or subtle, muted tones, the choice of paint can dramatically alter the appearance of the furniture and enhance the overall ambiance of your space.

Engaging in this DIY project allows you to embrace your creative side and enjoy the satisfaction that comes from making something uniquely yours. By taking the time to transform IKEA furniture with your personal touch, you are not just completing a task; you are embarking on a journey of artistic expression and home enhancement. Enjoy the process of making your IKEA hack truly your own, and revel in the knowledge that you have crafted a piece that is as functional as it is beautiful.

WHAT WOOD TO USE FOR FRAMING

When starting your upcoming IKEA hack project, choosing the appropriate material is crucial for combining functionality with style. Pine, among the many choices, is a standout option for DIY enthusiasts. Its affordability, versatility, and user-friendly nature make pine wood an ideal candidate for transforming standard IKEA furniture. Whether it's for a frame, base, or top piece, securing MDF onto pine is my preferred approach. You can find 2400mm lengths in-store for just a few pounds each.

WHAT MDF TO USE FOR FRAMING

MDF

If you're eager to transform your IKEA creations into sleek, modern masterpieces, Medium Density Fiberboard (MDF) is the material you want to explore. This versatile, cost-effective engineered wood is celebrated for its smooth surface and even texture, making it perfect for projects that demand a flawless paint finish or intricate detailing. With its consistent density and ease of cutting, MDF empowers DIY enthusiasts to make precise, polished modifications to standard IKEA items. Whether you're envisioning custom shelving, upgraded cabinet fronts, or unique decorative pieces, MDF offers a strong, durable foundation to fuel your creativity. In this guide, we'll dive into the benefits of using MDF for your IKEA hacks and show you how to find the highest-quality boards at your local DIY store.

You can conveniently purchase pre-cut MDF online or visit a local DIY store or builder's merchant equipped with a board cutting machine.

PROJECT PLANNER

Project Name

Start Date

End Date

Project Description

Must have features

Shopping list

Ideas & Notes

DESIGNING SHEET

PROJECT PLANNER

Project Name

Start Date

End Date

Project Description

Must have features

Shopping list

Ideas & Notes

DESIGNING SHEET

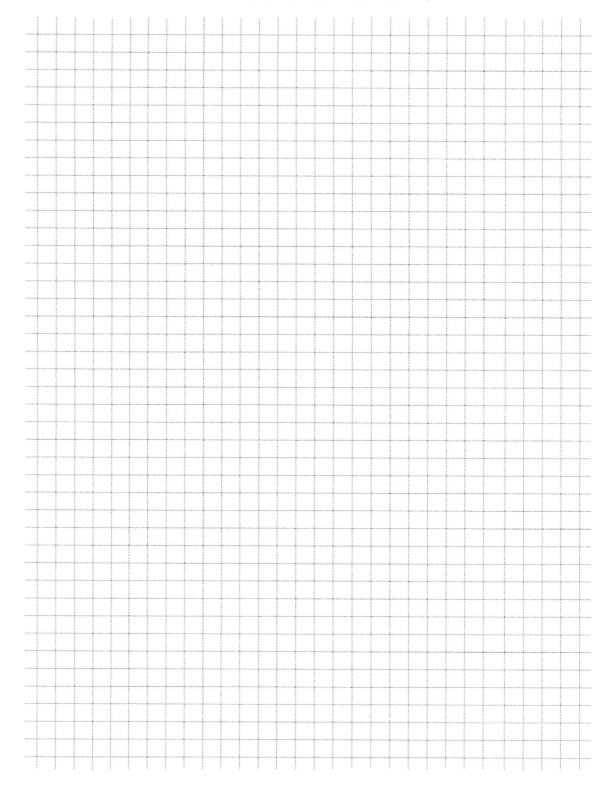

PROJECT PLANNER

Project Name

Start Date

End Date

Project Description

Must have features

Shopping list

Ideas & Notes

DESIGNING SHEET

PROJECT PLANNER

Project Name

Start Date

End Date

Project Description

Must have features

Shopping list

Ideas & Notes

DESIGNING SHEET

PROJECT PLANNER

Project Name

Start Date

End Date

Project Description

Must have features

Shopping list

Ideas & Notes

DESIGNING SHEET

GET READY TO GET HACKING

As we reach the end of this journey through the world of IKEA hacking, it's clear that the possibilities are as limitless as your imagination. This handbook was crafted not just as a guide to repurposing and personalizing IKEA products, but as an inspiration to look at the ordinary and see the extraordinary.

Throughout these pages, we've explored how simple modifications can transform basic furniture into something uniquely yours, reflecting your personal style and needs. We've seen how creativity, coupled with a bit of elbow grease, can turn a mass-produced item into a bespoke piece that tells a story.

But beyond the hacks and the transformations lies a deeper message: the power of creativity in our everyday lives. IKEA hacking is more than just a DIY trend; it's a movement that encourages us to think outside the box, to challenge the status quo, and to take ownership of our living spaces in innovative ways without breaking the bank.

As you continue your DIY adventures, remember that every project, no matter how small, contributes to a bigger narrative of creativity and resourcefulness. May this handbook serve as a springboard, sparking new ideas and projects that bring joy and functionality to your life.

Thank you for embarking on this creative journey with me. Now, armed with inspiration and knowledge, go forth and hack your world!

Kirsty x

HANDMADE WITH LOVE

Made in the USA
Columbia, SC
08 January 2025

51394915R00057